*Shakes
His Life and Plays*

WILL FOWLER

Level 4

Series Editors: Andy Hopkins and Jocelyn Potter

Pearson Education Limited
Edinburgh Gate, Harlow,
Essex CM20 2JE, England
and Associated Companies throughout the world.

ISBN 0997 805811

First published 2001
This edition published 2006

1 3 5 7 9 10 8 6 4 2

Text copyright © Will Fowler 2001

Typeset by Pantek Arts Ltd, Maidstone, Kent
Set in 11/14pt Bembo
Printed in China
SWTC/01

Published by Pearson Education Limited in association with Penguin
Books Ltd, both companies being subsidiaries of Pearson Plc

Photograph acknowledgements:
Robert Harding: pp. 2 and 7; Fotomas Index: p. 55
Donald Cooper/Photostage: pp. 12, 22, 25, 39, 43 and 51;

Portrait of Richard Burbage (1573-1619) (oil on canvas) by English School (17th Century)
(page 17): Dulwich Picture Gallery, London, UK/Bridgeman Art Library

Henry Wriothesky, 3rd Earl of Southampton (1573-1624), 1603
by John Decritz, the elder (c.1552-1642) (attr. to) (page 34): Boughton House,
Northamptonshire, UK/Bridgeman Art Library

For a complete list of titles available in the Penguin Readers series please write to your local
Pearson Education office or contact: Penguin Readers Marketing Department,
Pearson Education, Edinburgh Gate, Harlow, Essex, CM20 2JE.

Contents

Introduction

If you are fortunate enough to see a great Shakespeare play well acted, this is still the most wonderful experience that you can have in a theatre.

Almost everyone agrees that William Shakespeare is the greatest writer in the English language. He wrote more great plays of different kinds than anyone else in the world. But we do not know much more about his life than the information that we can find in legal documents. Most of the stories about his personal life were written long after his death and we cannot be sure that they are true. In an honest report of his life, the writer must often include the words 'perhaps' or 'probably'. Unlike his friend and rival, Ben Jonson, Shakespeare did not leave a notebook or publish his opinions on art or politics or religion. His only published personal poems, his Sonnets, show us his feelings about a man and a woman, but we are not sure who they were.

For this reason, and because Shakespeare was an actor and did not go to a university, people have tried to prove that someone else wrote the plays. But serious students agree that the opposite is true. Shakespeare became a great dramatist because he was a professional man of the theatre. He learnt to write plays by seeing and acting in plays written by others.

Shakespeare is the greatest of all dramatists because his characters seem real and he included all kinds of people. We laugh or suffer with them and leave the theatre happy or sad because of what we have learnt about life. Shakespeare's plays are not only great literature, but are alive after more than 400 years.

Chapter 1   Stratford Childhood

On or about 22 April 1564, Mary Arden, the wife of John Shakespeare, gave birth to a son in Stratford-upon-Avon. She had lost two baby girls before that. Now, all through the hot summer, she was afraid of losing her third child because there was a plague in Stratford. Her husband was a member of the town council, so they could not leave the town. By the end of the year, 300 of the population of 1,500 were dead, but fortunately for Mary and for us, her baby William did not die. He grew up, and became the greatest writer in the English language.

Mary was about twenty-four when he was born. She was the youngest of four daughters of a farmer near Stratford. Soon after her father died, in 1557, she married John Shakespeare, who was about ten years older. As a young man, John had worked on one of the Ardens' farms, but he had left the village and moved to Stratford. He learnt how to make gloves and other things from leather, and he became a successful businessman. A year before his marriage, he bought the two houses that are now known as Shakespeare's birthplace. The family lived in one and used the other as their shop.

Nobody can explain how ordinary parents produce sons like William Shakespeare. He had three younger brothers and a sister, but none of them did anything very important in life. But William became a good businessman, like his father, and his mother was clearly intelligent. Though she was the youngest daughter, her father had made her responsible for his will when he died and had left her his best property.

William's childhood was probably quite happy. His father's business was doing well and when William was four years old, John Shakespeare became the leader of the town council.

Shakespeare's birthplace in Stratford-upon-Avon

After Shakespeare's death, many stories were told about him that were not true. A long time afterwards, people began to wonder whether he had really written the plays. He had not been to a university like most other writers for the theatre in those days. Shakespeare's friend and rival, Ben Jonson, was partly responsible for this doubt. He said that Shakespeare was the greatest of all dramatists, although he 'had small Latin and less Greek'. These were the main subjects that boys studied at school. But Jonson had been one of the best students at a famous school. So when he compared himself with Shakespeare, 'small Latin and less Greek' only meant that Jonson knew a lot more.

In fact, William's school in Stratford was a good one. From the age of nine or ten, all the lessons there were in Latin, and the boys stayed until they were fifteen. We can also see from studying the sources of his plays that Shakespeare could certainly read

Latin and could also read French and Italian. But the plays are clearly the work of a professional man of the theatre. This is the real answer to the question: 'Did Shakespeare write them?'

William's last years at school were probably not as happy as the early ones. From 1576, when he was twelve, his father stopped going to council meetings. Perhaps he was ashamed to meet his friends; his business was not going so well. In 1579 he borrowed money from one of his wife's relatives, who took a house and land in exchange. He could not pay the money back on the date that they had agreed, and afterwards the man refused to take it. He preferred to keep the property. This house and land had belonged to Mary's family, and William tried for many years to get them back but was not successful.

There was, perhaps, another reason why John Shakespeare did not go to council meetings. We need to know something about the political and religious history of England in the sixteenth century to understand it. In those days, religion always played a very important part in politics.

Henry VIII, who was King of England from 1509 to 1547, had married a Spanish princess, Catherine of Aragon. They had a daughter, Mary, but Henry wanted a son so he asked the Pope* to end his marriage. The Pope refused. He knew that Charles, the King of Spain, would be angry at this insult to his aunt. So Henry made himself the head of the new Church of England and married Anne Boleyn. When she could only give him another daughter, he executed her. His third wife, Jane Seymour, gave him the son that he desired, but she died soon afterwards.

This son, Edward, became king when he was ten years old. His mother's relatives were Protestants, so the country changed from being almost Catholic (but without the Pope) to Protestant. But

*The Pope: the head of the Catholic church.

3

when Edward died six years later, his sister Mary became queen. She was a very religious woman. She married her Catholic cousin, Philip II, the King of Spain, and burnt Protestants to death. Five years later she died, and Anne Boleyn's daughter, Elizabeth, who had been in prison, became queen.

People wondered if Elizabeth would marry a foreign king or prince, like her sister. He would probably be a Catholic. Or would she marry the man that she loved, the Earl of Leicester, who was a Protestant? Nobody imagined that a woman could govern the country alone. In fact, she never married, but was Queen of England for nearly fifty years.

Religion mattered less to Elizabeth than politics. English people were worried that the wars between different members of the royal family would return. Elizabeth wanted peace. She expected everyone to go to church on Sundays, but she did not mind if they were still Catholics at home.

By 1579, when William Shakespeare left school, things had changed. Catholics had rebelled against the queen. They aimed to make her cousin, Mary, Queen of Scots, queen. Mary had lost her throne and was in prison in England. England was not yet at war with Spain but Elizabeth supported men like Francis Drake, who attacked Spanish ships carrying gold from America.

Shakespeare's mother's family, the Ardens, were Catholics. A document was found in the roof of his birthplace many years after his death which suggests that John Shakespeare was privately a Catholic, too. Elizabeth did not execute Catholics for their religion – only if they were politically dangerous. But it is easy for people in a small town to invent stories about their neighbours. Perhaps John Shakespeare stayed away from council meetings because he was afraid that someone would ask him about his religion. But he was a popular man. His friends kept him on the council for ten years after he stopped going to the meetings.

It is unlikely that William thought of being an actor or of writing plays at this time. The theatre was not a profession for gentlemen. Actors were either employed by lords and rich men to entertain them and their guests, or they travelled around the country, performing plays if the council allowed it. Most councils refused permission. Actors did not earn their living just by acting, either. They were expected to dance and sing, to tell jokes and perform tricks.

There was a great tradition of acting in England, but the actors were not professionals. In big cities groups still performed religious plays on Corpus Christi★ day every summer. Shakespeare saw them when he was young because Coventry, near Stratford, was the last city where they were performed. But Protestants did not celebrate Corpus Christi, and the government thought that the plays kept the old religion alive. They did not punish anyone for performing them. They just asked for the play books to check that there was nothing in them against Protestant beliefs, and forgot to give them back. Later, the books were usually destroyed.

At that time, the professional theatre was only just beginning and there were very few plays for actors to perform. The first real theatre in London opened in 1576. The owner and builder was James Burbage. Years later, his son Richard played the hero in all of Shakespeare's greatest successes.

Chapter 2   A Wife and Children

We do not hear of Shakespeare again until 1582, when he married Anne Hathaway. But there is an interesting story about

★Corpus Christi: Latin for 'Body of Christ'; a Catholic celebration.

him that may explain what he did after leaving school. John Aubrey, writing about a hundred years later, did not agree with Ben Jonson's report that Shakespeare had 'small Latin'. He says that Shakespeare 'understood Latin well' because he had been a teacher in the country when he was young. This story may be true because it was told by William Beeston, the son of one of the actors in Shakespeare's theatre company.

Shakespeare was not a professional teacher but young men sometimes worked privately in rich men's houses, teaching their families or servants. There is a tradition in a family called Hoghton in Lancashire that Shakespeare worked for them for two years. The Hoghtons were Catholics and rich enough to have their own group of actors. When Alexander Hoghton died in 1581, he left the actors' clothes and musical instruments to his brother. He asked him to employ two men who had lived with him, or to help them find work, and one of those men was called William Shakeshaft.

It is unusual to speak of a servant 'living with' a family, and so it seems that these two men had special jobs. Shakeshaft and Shakespeare mean the same thing and in those days people often confused names or copied them down wrongly. We cannot prove that Shakespeare taught in the Hoghton house or that he had his first experience of theatre there. But it is interesting that the earls of Derby were among the Hoghtons' neighbours, and the families were friends. When Shakespeare joined his first theatre company in London, it was probably Strange's. The company's patron was Lord Ferdinando Strange, the Earl of Derby's son.

We do not know whether Shakespeare went to Lancashire or stayed at home to help his father with his business. But in the summer of 1582, he was certainly in Stratford. Then, if not before, he began to walk across the fields to the village of Shottery to see Anne Hathaway. Shakespeare was only eighteen, and Anne was twenty-six or twenty-seven, so some writers

Anne Hathaway's house in the village of Shottery

imagine that she tricked him into marrying her. But Shakespeare's Sonnets – about 150 short poems, published in 1609 – are our only guide to his private thoughts and feelings. They tell a different story.

Shakespeare and other Elizabethan poets were fond of using words with two meanings, or words that sounded similar. In one of the sonnets, he suggests Anne's surname with the words 'hate away'. The poem is about a young man, excited and in love, and a girl who at first says no to him but then pities him and says that she loves him.

Anne's father had died the year before, leaving her some money for the day when she got married. He had married twice and Anne, the oldest daughter of the first marriage, had to help his second wife look after her four young children. Anne probably found the clever young man attractive and wanted to have her own children. She had known Shakespeare since he was a boy. Many years before, John Shakespeare had helped her father when Mr Hathaway could not pay his bills. William Shakespeare, at this time, was probably a young man in search of romantic experience.

In November, when Anne was expecting a baby, the couple were given special permission to get married the next day. Shakespeare was under the age of twenty-one, so he also needed his father's permission. Perhaps Shakespeare's parents did not agree to the marriage until they were sure of Anne's condition. Towards the end of May 1583, Anne gave birth to a daughter, Susanna. There is reason to believe that Susanna was the person that Shakespeare loved most and the member of his family who was most like him.

For the next two years at least, the young couple lived with Shakespeare's parents. At the end of January 1585, they had twins, a boy and a girl. They called them Hamnet and Judith after their friends Hamnet Sadler, the baker, and his wife. Most Elizabethan wives had children almost every year, so it is a little surprising that Shakespeare and Anne had only three. It is true that he was not often at home after he moved to London, though he probably returned to Stratford once a year. It is also possible that Anne could not have more children after she had twins; in those days it was more difficult and dangerous to give birth than it is now.

During this time, we suppose that Shakespeare helped his father. It was useful for a businessman to have a son who could read and write. But it is unlikely that Shakespeare wanted to spend the rest of his life in Stratford, making gloves.

We do not know when or why he left the town. He probably went to London a year or two after the twins were born. Perhaps he carried with him a letter to Lord Strange's company of actors from friends in Lancashire. Long after his death Nicholas Rowe, who wrote the first life of Shakespeare, said that he had to leave Stratford. It was a punishment for hunting in a park that belonged to Sir Thomas Lucy. If the story is true, Shakespeare took his revenge in *The Merry Wives of Windsor*, a play that contains many memories of his childhood. Lucy was a judge in Stratford and Shallow, the foolish country judge in the play, may be like him.

Chapter 3   The Lost Years

No one has solved the mystery of the lost years in Shakespeare's life, the years between 1585 and 1592. We can only imagine what happened before we first hear of him as a dramatist.

The first person to write about Shakespeare's plays criticized him. Robert Greene, a successful dramatist, was dying in the autumn of 1592. His last work contains an angry personal attack on Shakespeare. We learn from it that Shakespeare was an actor. He had also certainly written three plays and probably as many as seven or eight. He had therefore worked in the theatre for a number of years and had started writing plays not long after he joined a theatre company.

Greene attacks Shakespeare for two reasons. At that time, plays were usually written by men like himself who had been to a university. Greene wants to warn other dramatists of the danger to their profession if actors like Shakespeare are allowed to write plays. His more serious complaint is that Shakespeare has copied their work. He compares him to a bird that copies the sounds made by other birds.

It is unlikely that Greene really believed that Shakespeare copied other writers' speeches. He was angry because he realized that Shakespeare had borrowed their ideas and used those ideas to write better plays. By 1592, Shakespeare was already very successful, and had succeeded with different kinds of play – plays about English history, comedies and a tragedy. Greene complains that this young man thinks that he can do everything in the theatre.

We can understand Greene's attitude better if we compare the theatre in London in Shakespeare's time to Hollywood in the 1930s. The situation was similar in many ways. The actors were the stars. Everyone in London knew the name of Edward Alleyn, the most famous actor at that time. But the dramatists were like the people who wrote the 1930s films. Their names did not appear outside the theatre, and the manager of the company often made them write in small teams to produce plays faster. Films in Hollywood were written in this way when the cinema was the main form of popular entertainment. When the writers sold their work to a theatre company, they lost control over it. Plays were not usually published because that allowed rival companies to perform them. The company only published them if it needed money or if someone had produced a bad copy of one. Only half of Shakespeare's thirty-seven plays were printed in his lifetime.

It seems surprising that the world's greatest dramatist did not take more care of his work. To understand that, we must again make a comparison with Hollywood. Until the 1950s, the films of great directors like John Ford or Howard Hawks were not accepted as art. In the same way, during the twenty-five years of Shakespeare's life in the theatre, plays were not 'literature'. Shakespeare probably accepted the general opinion. He published his poems, which in his opinion proved his ability as a writer.

His first plays show that he was still learning. Christopher Marlowe, who was the same age as Shakespeare but had started earlier, was a greater poet at this time, and his plays had made Edward Alleyn a star. Thomas Kyd had written the most exciting play of the 1580s, *The Spanish Tragedy*. People today think that Shakespeare stood alone, far above the other dramatists of his time, but many of them wrote excellent plays that are still performed.

Shakespeare's greatest strength was his willingness to try new ideas. He remembered the Latin comedies of Plautus and Terence and the tragedies of Seneca that he had studied at school, and copied them. He studied the plays of his rivals and the changing fashions among the audience. When he was the most successful dramatist in London, he used the subjects of old plays that he had seen or acted in and produced something much better. Even his own tragedies and comedies are different from each other. Most dramatists repeat their successes. Shakespeare only seemed to write the same kind of play if he was not satisfied at first. Then he continued until he got it right.

The early plays are therefore very different from each other, as Shakespeare tried one form after another. He wrote three plays about the wars in England in the fifteenth century, and another play about English history. There was a Roman tragedy that is so violent that many people would like to believe he did not write it. And he wrote three comedies – a romantic comedy, a comedy taken from Plautus, and one that uses familiar scenes from Stratford.

The most interesting are the last two, *The Comedy of Errors* and *The Taming of the Shrew*. The first is the story of a man and his servant. They were lost when they were babies and arrive in a town where each one has a twin brother with the same name. It is one of the funniest plays that Shakespeare wrote. He makes clever use of all the possibilities for confusion. Antipholus of Syracuse, the recently arrived brother, cannot understand why a strange woman – Adriana, his brother's wife – is angry with him. When he falls in love with her sister, Luciana, he is surprised that she is shocked and upset.

The Taming of the Shrew is often criticized today. It seems to be about a man who marries a bad-tempered girl and is cruel to her until she is willing to obey him. The play is one of a number that modern audiences are unwilling to accept. We should not be

The Taming of the Shrew *tries to show that in a good marriage the two people are partners and work together as a team.*

surprised that Shakespeare did not always have the same view of life as we have, since he died nearly 400 years ago. But the real problem is often that the modern director does not understand the play and introduces his own ideas.

Shakespeare did not usually give the Elizabethan audience just what they expected, either. There were hundreds of stories about bad-tempered women in Europe, but *The Taming of the Shrew* is not typical of them. It tries to show that in a good marriage the two people are partners and work together as a team. The wife does not always have to obey her husband, as most of the audience believed.

Chapter 4   Plague, Poems and a Patron

When Robert Greene wrote his attack on Shakespeare in 1592, the theatres were closed. The plague had returned to London that summer and the future for a dramatist was uncertain. Who could say when the theatres would open again? In fact, they were closed all through the following year, and by the spring of 1594 the actors were in serious trouble.

Most writers at that time needed a patron. A lord like Lord Ferdinando Strange sometimes gave his name to a company of actors, but poets were the only writers who could hope for support. No help was given to dramatists. So, in the spring of 1593, Shakespeare wrote a poem, *Venus and Adonis*, and published it with a letter to Henry Wriothesley, Earl of Southampton. We cannot be sure that he knew the Earl at this time, but it seems likely that they met and that Southampton invited him to his country house in Hampshire. Shakespeare's second long poem, *The Rape of Lucrece*, was published in the following year. In it he says that his love for the Earl 'is without end', and promises that his past and future work is for his patron.

The relationship between Shakespeare and Southampton has been a cause of argument. Was the Earl the handsome young man who appears in the Sonnets? In these poems, the poet loves him but the young man takes a dark-haired woman from him. We shall never know. Southampton was certainly handsome, and people said that he had physical relationships with other men, which was a crime in those days. When Shakespeare published *Venus and Adonis*, Southampton was only twenty years old.

The political connections are more important. Southampton was a close friend of the Earl of Essex, a favourite of Queen Elizabeth and the leader of a political party. Essex continually criticized the government of Lord Burghley, who had been the Queen's first minister since the beginning of her reign. After 1594, Shakespeare's theatre company supported Essex, and they were very lucky to escape punishment when he was executed in 1601. Southampton, too, was fortunate to be sent to prison instead of dying with him.

There are two reasons for believing that Shakespeare spent time as a guest in Southampton's house in 1593. First, during that time he wrote a play called *Love's Labour's Lost*. He usually used stories by other people as a starting point, but on three occasions in the 1590s the story was the product of his own imagination. These plays were written for special occasions, though they were all performed in the public theatre later.

Love's Labour's Lost is full of the kind of romantic language that lords and ladies liked to hear, but there are also a few political jokes and characters who make fun of other writers. The story begins with the real meeting some years before between the Protestant King of Navarre (by 1593 Henry IV, King of France) and the Princess of France. The King's followers in the play, Biron and Longueville, have the names of the lords who were with him when the Earl of Essex met Henry in France in 1591. It seems likely that the play was written for a private performance at Southampton's house while the theatres were closed because of the plague.

After Queen Elizabeth's death in 1603, King James I freed Southampton from prison and he soon became the favourite dancing partner of the new queen, Anna of Denmark. In the winter of 1604–5, Shakespeare's company performed at court eleven times. Southampton probably chose the plays, eight of them by Shakespeare. Most of them were his more recent successes, but among them was *Love's Labour's Lost*. It seems a strange choice unless Southampton was celebrating his good luck and remembered its first performance in happier times many years earlier.

Even if Shakespeare spent some time in Southampton's house in 1593–4, the young lord could not give him much help. He had annoyed Lord Burghley by refusing to marry his granddaughter, and had spent most of his money. It seems that Southampton continued to think well of Shakespeare, but Shakespeare had to return to the theatre to earn his living.

◆

The future of the theatre in England in the spring of 1594 was very uncertain. Marlowe was dead. According to the official report, he had an argument with another man over a bill in a pub and was killed, but the man was not punished. The other man was a government spy, and Marlowe had also worked as a spy. Modern writers suggest that Marlowe was killed because he liked to shock people and knew too many of the government's secrets.

On 16 April 1594, Lord Ferdinando Strange died suddenly. He had been the patron of the company that Shakespeare had probably joined when he came to London. People said that the government had poisoned Strange because some Catholics wanted him to be king. His company had divided in two in 1591, when Edward Alleyn had had an argument with James Burbage. Alleyn and some other actors had left Burbage's theatre, taking some of the play books with them, and had joined a rival theatre owner, Philip Henslowe. Lord Strange had continued to be the patron of this group. While the theatres were closed, Alleyn had married Henslowe's daughter. Shakespeare probably stayed with the Burbage family at first, and for a time the Earl of Pembroke was their patron.

In 1593, during the time of the plague, the two companies went on tours of the country. The Pembrokes' tour was a disaster and the actors lost everything. Shakespeare was not with them, perhaps because he was staying with the Earl of Southampton.

It seemed that the theatre in London would come to an end because there was no one to support it. Then the government saved it. It was fortunate for Elizabethan actors, and for us, that the Queen was very fond of plays. Every year she liked to see performances at court at Christmas time. The city council often asked the government to close the theatres, but they were always told that they had to keep them open. The actors needed to practise before performing in front of the Queen.

The government formed two new companies, and each had a patron. One company, acting at Henslowe's theatre, was led by Edward Alleyn. Shakespeare returned to the other company at Burbage's theatre. The leading actor there was Burbage's son, Richard, and its patron was Lord Hunsdon.

Lord Hunsdon was the Queen's cousin and an important man at court. He was an old man, but was a good friend to the actors. Shakespeare chose wisely when he joined Burbage. James Burbage, like Henslowe, often cheated the actors, but his son Richard was Shakespeare's friend. When his father died, Shakespeare became one of the partners in the company.

Shakespeare wrote for the actors that he knew and his plays are the result of working as part of a team. So it is important for us that Burbage was a more interesting actor than Alleyn and spent his whole life in the theatre. Alleyn left the stage in 1597

Richard Burbage was Shakespeare's friend – and one of the leading actors in Shakespeare's theatre.

and grew rich as Henslowe's partner. Burbage was still acting in the year of his death, three years after Shakespeare in 1619.

Alleyn and Burbage were similar to the two leading actors in Shakespeare's plays in England in the twentieth century, John Gielgud and Laurence Olivier. Alleyn, like Gielgud, had a beautiful voice. He was at his best in the long speeches that Marlowe wrote for him. They were fine words but did not demand much movement. Burbage, like Olivier, was more active on the stage and could play many different parts.

We do not know if Shakespeare had written *Richard III* before the theatres closed. He had already invented the character of this wonderful villain in the last part of his history play, *Henry VI*. It was the perfect part for Burbage, as it was hundreds of years later for Laurence Olivier. As usual, Shakespeare had copied another writer and improved his work. Richard is like the Jew of Malta in Marlowe's play of that name, but Shakespeare's play is better. The audience watch, half shocked and half amused, as the villain comes to the front of the stage – in the Elizabethan theatre he was in the middle of them – and tells them his plans. Then they watch, half shocked and half excited, to see if he will succeed.

Chapter 5   Great Success and a Personal Tragedy

In the next four years, between 1594 and 1598, Shakespeare wrote eight plays and became the leading dramatist of his time. The first three, *Richard II*, *Romeo and Juliet* and *A Midsummer Night's Dream*, show that the years of writing poems were still very much in his mind. Two are tragedies, and the third is a comedy specially written for the wedding of Lord Hunsdon's granddaughter in 1596. But all three are still loved above all for the beauty of the language. While Laurence Olivier's best part was Richard III, John Gielgud's was Richard II.

Even in these plays we can see how Shakespeare's skill in the theatre was growing. In *Romeo and Juliet*, the scenes between the lovers are full of beautiful speeches. But Shakespeare also included the practical words of the Nurse, who came straight from his Stratford childhood, and the rather different ways of speaking of Mercutio and Capulet, Juliet's father. He was beginning to give each character a personal voice.

A Midsummer Night's Dream is perhaps the loveliest play that Shakespeare wrote. Shakespeare invented three stories and put them together cleverly as the perfect entertainment for a wedding. One is about young lovers, as usual unwilling to obey their parents' wishes; another is about the fairy king and queen, who use their magic power to confuse the lovers; the third is about a group of actors who are going to perform a play for the wedding of Theseus, the Duke of Athens, and Hippolyta.

Professional actors enjoy making fun of ordinary people trying to act. *A Midsummer Night's Dream* contains a number of jokes about Shakespeare and his friends. The actors in the play perform a tragedy about two young lovers, like Shakespeare's last play, *Romeo and Juliet*, but their performance is full of comic mistakes. The leading actor, Bottom, is like many stars in the theatre. He wants to play all the parts himself. In *A Midsummer Night's Dream*, though, for the first time, Shakespeare suggests that he was beginning to think of plays as art. His character Theseus says that poets are like mad people; they imagine things that are not real. But Hippolyta answers that the audience have seen a dream which has the power to stay in the mind afterwards. We can recognize that something is true more easily in art than in real life.

At one time it was thought that Shakespeare planned to write a group of four plays about English history in the early fifteenth century. But the plays are very different from each other, so it seems that he wrote them one by one. *Richard II* is the tragedy of a man with little political ability who becomes king. His cousin,

Bolingbroke, rebelled against him and became king in his place as Henry IV. Soon afterwards, Richard was murdered in prison and Henry's supporters in the north, the Percy family, rebelled against him.

In 1596, Shakespeare had a good reason for writing a play on this subject. The Percy family were Catholics, and many years earlier the company's patron, Lord Hunsdon, had fought against them and beaten them when they had rebelled against his cousin, the Queen. When they watched *Richard II*, the audience were sure to think of the Queen and her cousin.

Many people in the audience also remembered two plays about the reigns of Henry IV and Henry V that had been very popular a few years before. These plays were really both about Henry V, the greatest English war leader in history at that time. He had got into trouble as a young man because he had a friend called Sir John Oldcastle and they behaved badly. When he became king, he changed completely and was remembered afterwards as a hero.

At first, Shakespeare planned to write two plays like this, one about Henry V while he was still a prince, the other about him as king. But when he invented the character of the Prince's friend, Oldcastle, he saw that it was the perfect part for one of the stars of his company, the comic actor, Will Kempe. As in many other plays, he used two similar stories for comparison; here, one is serious and one is comic. The relationship between the Prince and Oldcastle tells us something about the relationship between the Prince and his father. But because the two stories are both very interesting, Shakespeare realized that he had too much to say for one play, so he divided the first play, called *Henry IV*, in two.

This was not the end of the matter. *Henry IV Part I* was acted with great success, but soon afterwards Lord Hunsdon died and Lord Cobham took his place at the royal court. Lord Cobham belonged to the Oldcastle family. He complained that the company were making fun of Oldcastle, so Shakespeare had to change the name. This is why one of his most famous characters is called Falstaff.

There is a story that Queen Elizabeth enjoyed the play so much that she wanted to see a play about Falstaff in love. Lord Cobham died in March, and Lord Hunsdon's son took his position. He was going to join the Queen for a celebration at Windsor that summer. Shakespeare had started writing *Henry IV Part II*, but he had to stop and write a special entertainment, *The Merry Wives of Windsor*. It is said that he wrote it in two weeks.

The play is very funny and has a lot of characters with amusing accents. One of them is a Welsh teacher, who is annoyed with a little boy called William in a Latin lesson. Here Shakespeare was remembering his childhood. As usual, he used the experience to improve his next play.

Henry IV Part II is not really a history play. Falstaff and his men appear in most of the scenes, which clearly take place in the England of Shakespeare's own time. The play suggests that the great days of the past have ended. Many people felt like that towards the end of the great queen's reign. Falstaff in this play is not so amusing. He is old and tired and cheats simple country people like the judge, Shallow, while he is waiting for the Prince to become king. Then he hopes that he will be a favourite at court. But at the end of the play, the new king, Henry V, gives him money but says that he must stay away from him.

Falstaff is the first of Shakespeare's characters who is so interesting on the stage that he has a life outside the theatre. People have heard of him before they see or read the play. This situation began 200 years ago, when it became the custom to talk about characters in plays as real people. And so today we may see *Henry IV Part II* performed with the Prince as a kind of villain. The director thinks that the audience will feel more sorry for Falstaff and blame the Prince for what happens to him. The same

Falstaff is one of Shakespeare's most famous characters.

custom is the reason why Shylock, the villain in *The Merchant of Venice*, is often changed into a man who is unfairly punished, and Hamlet becomes a sad dreamer who cannot make up his mind.

Although Shakespeare understood life better than most of his audience, he belonged to his own time. We cannot always expect him to think in the same way as we do. *The Merchant of Venice* is a typical example of this. Modern audiences feel guilty if they see a Jew as a villain because of the suffering of the Jewish people under Hitler. But in 1597 there were very few Jewish people in London, and they were not popular because most people thought that they had killed Jesus Christ.

Shakespeare wrote this play because the rival company had had a great success the year before with new performances of Marlowe's *The Jew of Malta*, written a few years earlier. Barabas, the Jew in Marlowe's play, is a villain like Richard III, with a cruel sense of humour. Burbage probably asked Shakespeare to write a part for him as good as that.

Shakespeare found an Italian story about a businessman in Venice who borrowed money from a Jew to help his nephew. The young man hoped to marry a rich woman. The businessman signed a document which allowed the Jew to cut him with a knife if he did not pay on time. There was nothing in the story about revenge. In Shakespeare's play Portia, the rich woman, becomes a beautiful young girl in love with the nephew, Bassanio. Antonio, the businessman, is Bassanio's friend, not his uncle.

Shylock's behaviour is in the old religious tradition of revenge ('an eye for an eye'), while Portia argues for Christian mercy and forgiveness. But in the great trial scene she has to win according to the law. The document allows Shylock to cut Antonio with his knife, and he chooses to do this near Antonio's heart. But it does not say anything about blood. Shylock loses because Antonio must not lose a drop of blood when he cuts him.

But Shylock is not the devil with red hair that Elizabethan audiences expected. He is given a great speech to prove that Jews are human like Christians, not devils. Shakespeare's understanding of people of all kinds allows him to make Shylock a real character and explain his behaviour. But this does not make him right. He uses the speech as an excuse for taking his revenge.

◆

During this busy time in the theatre, there was tragedy at home in Stratford. Shakespeare's only son, Hamnet, died in August 1596 at the age of eleven. We do not know how Shakespeare felt but it surely affected his view of life. Two months after that, he was given a coat of arms, which was the sign of a gentleman. His father had asked for one a long time before, when he was the leader of the council in Stratford. John Shakespeare was probably pleased, but William made a joke about it in *The Merry Wives of Windsor*. It would not now belong to his family after his own death, though, because he had no son to follow him.

We do not know anything about Shakespeare's private life in London. Stories about him suggest that he lived quietly and did not go out with other actors, drinking and looking for women. But the more powerful sonnets were probably written at this time, and they suggest that at times he felt guilty. One of the greatest of them, Sonnet 129, is about sex. All men know, he says, that sex without love seems attractive but afterwards they are ashamed of it. But although they know this, they cannot stop themselves doing it.

Shakespeare's success in the theatre had made him rich. His son was dead but he now had even more reason to take care of his wife and daughters. Early in 1597, he bought New Place, the second largest house in Stratford. Anne and their daughters moved there later in the year, while his parents stayed at the house where Shakespeare was born.

Shylock's speech proves that Jews are human like Christians.

Chapter 6   The Globe Theatre

During 1598, Shakespeare wrote another comedy that is still popular today, *Much Ado About Nothing*. As usual, he used two stories for a comparison. He took one couple, Claudio and Hero, from an Italian story. They have traditional ideas of love and arranged marriage. He invented the other couple, Beatrice and Benedick. They learn that real love is the product of what he calls in one of his sonnets, 'the marriage of true minds'. The character of the comic town policeman, Dogberry, comes from his Stratford childhood.

Everything seemed to be going well for the company. James Burbage was dead, and the company now belonged to his sons, Richard and Cuthbert. But in the cold winter of 1598, they had problems. The theatre stood inside the city of London, and the owner of the land refused to let them continue there. They had to perform a number of times at court at Christmas time, and for a month or two they acted in another, smaller building. Then the brothers reached a brave decision. Between their performances at court they took the whole wooden theatre, in pieces, across the river to some land outside the city. In the spring they built a new theatre and called it the Globe. The Burbages needed money and so they invited the five leading members of the company to join them. From this time, Shakespeare was a partner in the theatre.

For the new theatre, Shakespeare wrote three plays. He finished *Henry V* to complete the story of the Prince, and he also produced a comedy, *As You Like It*, and a tragedy, *Julius Caesar*.

Laurence Olivier made a great film of *Henry V* at the end of the Second World War. He was able to show the scenes of fighting in colour in the film. Shakespeare realized how difficult it would be to do this on the stage, so he wrote speeches – which he probably spoke himself – asking the audience to use their imagination.

In an Elizabethan theatre, they always had to do this. The theatre was outdoors and some of the audience stood around the stage in the open air. People could pay more money for seats at the sides. If they wanted to be seen, not to see the play, they could pay to sit on the stage itself.

There were only two entrances, both at the back of the stage, but there was a special door in the floor where characters like ghosts and devils could suddenly appear. But although the actors had some simple pieces of furniture, the audience had to imagine where the scene was taking place. The dramatist also had to remember that the actors would not always perform in a theatre. They often performed at court. If there was plague in the city and they had to go on tour, they had to act in any building that they could find.

Unlike most other dramatists, Shakespeare acted in the plays himself. This was a great advantage. While he was writing, he imagined where the actors would be. His plays are full of lines that tell the audience what is happening and show the actors what to do. The main story of his beautiful comedy, *As You Like It*, comes from a popular book by Thomas Lodge. Early in the play the heroine, Rosalind, and her cousin, Celia, go to the forest to look for Rosalind's father. Perhaps the actors put up two or three trees on the stage, but the audience knew that the girls had arrived when Rosalind said, 'Well, this is the forest of Arden.'

In the same way, Shakespeare told the audience when characters were coming on the stage or going off. He gave them a picture of the scene and told them the time. Plays at the Globe were acted in the afternoon, but the first scene of *Hamlet* begins at midnight and ends as Horatio describes the sun coming up over a hill in the east.

Although it may seem that the audience had to use their imagination all the time, Elizabethan theatres had one great advantage when compared with most theatres today. The stage

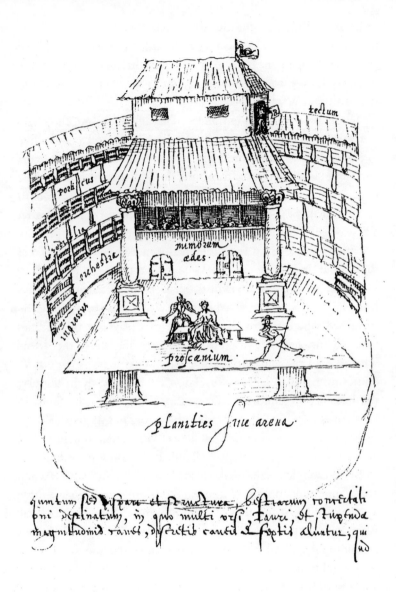

tectum

porticus

mimorum
ædes

orchestra

ingressus

proscænium

planities siue arena.

quintum ... sppara et ... ..., bestiarum ...
oni de ..., in quo multi vrsi, tauri, et ...
magnitudinis canes, ... cautis et septis aluntur, qui
ad

An Elizabethan theatre, drawn in 1596

area was much bigger, and the actors could stand in the middle of the audience. It was easier for a character like Richard III or Hamlet to make the audience believe that the other actors on the stage could not hear him. He was much nearer to the audience than to them. In the second scene of *Hamlet,* at least ten actors came on to the stage. They placed thrones for the King and Queen, and stood near them while Claudius made a long political speech. Everyone was dressed in bright colours to celebrate the wedding of Claudius and Gertrude except Hamlet, who was dressed in black. He stood at the front of the stage, as far from the King and Queen as possible, and told the audience what he thought of them.

The Globe immediately became the most popular theatre in London. In September 1599 a Swiss visitor, Thomas Platter, saw a performance of *Julius Caesar* there. His diary gives us an idea of what an Elizabethan performance was like. Even after a tragedy, the actors danced: 'I saw the tragedy of Julius Caesar with at least fifteen characters very well acted. At the end they danced according to their custom.'

Chapter 7   *Hamlet*, the Last Comedy and a Lucky Escape

Hamlet is probably Shakespeare's greatest play. It is certainly the most famous. But today's Hamlets are usually very different from each other and from the one that Shakespeare wrote about in 1600.

Goethe began this fashion 200 years ago. He said that Hamlet was a gentle young man, unable to obey his father's command that he must revenge his murder. After that, it was easy to imagine that he was a man who could not make up his mind. But to some modern writers Hamlet is cruel and violent and not really the hero. Others have suggested that Hamlet's relationship with his mother is the most important point in the play. It is also often difficult today to know whether the actor thinks that Hamlet is really mad or is only pretending to be.

Shakespeare had seen a play about Hamlet when he first came to London, probably written by Thomas Kyd. We only know that Kyd's play had a ghost who called for revenge. But there was probably a scene like the one where the actors act the murder of Hamlet's father, proving that Claudius is guilty. Kyd had a scene like this in *The Spanish Tragedy*. Shakespeare had also read the story in a translation from the French, and had studied a medical book. He had to show the difference between someone who really goes mad, like Ophelia, and someone like Hamlet who has suffered a shock but at times pretends to be mad to trick his enemies.

Here are a few short answers to the problems that modern directors have with *Hamlet*. Officially, Protestants like Hamlet's friend, Horatio, did not believe in ghosts for religious reasons. So when the Ghost first appears, Horatio is sure that it is the Devil. Hamlet thinks that it may be the Devil, so he has to wait until he can prove that the King is guilty before taking his revenge. He sees his opportunity, halfway through the play, when he asks the actors to perform a play with a scene like his father's murder. But even then, only he and Horatio understand why the King is shocked. If they have not read the story, the audience do not know if the Ghost is the Devil, either, until just before that scene. After that, Hamlet acts immediately, but by mistake kills the minister – Polonius, Ophelia's father – instead of the King. He does not have another opportunity until the end of the play.

Polonius's death is the cause of the tragedy. Ophelia goes mad and her brother, Laertes, when he returns from France, is in the same situation as Hamlet. The King blames Hamlet, and Laertes wants revenge. He is more typical of an Elizabethan gentleman than Hamlet. He does not stop to find out if the King's story is true. He says that he will cut Hamlet's throat in the church.

The Elizabethan audience shared Hamlet's view of his mother's marriage to his uncle. For them, this was the same as a man marrying his sister. So when the King, pretending that he is Hamlet's friend, calls him 'my cousin [relative] and my son', Hamlet turns away from him. He tells the audience that the King is closer than a relative but less than natural.

Elizabethan audiences were never in doubt about Hamlet's madness. Shakespeare used different forms of language for his speeches. These showed clearly when he was shocked by his father's death and his mother's marriage and when he was pretending.

Most audiences admire Hamlet. But it is true that he changes during the play. We admire the Hamlet that we see at the end. Then he speaks calmly to Horatio, saying that the opportunity to revenge his father will come in time, and he will be ready. We should also recognize that the tradition in revenge plays is similar to the tradition in a Western★ film. The villain had to be the cause of his own death. In the same way, the bad man in a Western always reaches for his gun first, before the hero shoots him. If the hero shot first, we would not like it.

Shakespeare gives us his idea of Hamlet in the words of Ophelia. When she thinks that he is mad, she speaks of him as he was before the play began and as he is again at the end. He is the perfect Elizabethan prince, a man who knows how to behave in society, who reads books to increase his knowledge of the world, and who will fight bravely when this is necessary.

At this time, Shakespeare also wrote *Twelfth Night*, his last romantic comedy. It is a fine play, with wonderfully funny scenes

★Western: a film about heroes and villains in the western United States, with stars like John Wayne and Clint Eastwood.

and beautiful romantic speeches. But there is a kind of sadness about it that lasts even after the happy ending. Orsino, the hero, is in love with the idea of love, but Viola, the heroine, is really in love. She acts as Orsino's servant for most of the play, dressed as a boy. In the end, we feel that he does not really deserve her.

At the end of *Twelfth Night* Feste, one of the main comic characters in the play, sings a song. Will Kempe had left the company and a different actor, Robert Armin, who could sing well, had taken his place. Shakespeare wrote the comic parts in his plays to suit him. The meaning of Feste's song is not clear, but it may be about an actor's life. It is a hard life. The wind blows and the rain falls every day. When Feste sings about men shutting their gates against thieves, we remember that councils disliked actors and wanted to shut them out. But at the end of the song, Feste tells the audience that they will try to please them every day.

John Manningham, a law student, kept a diary. Law students in London were fond of plays and could afford to pay the actors to put on special performances for them. Manningham saw *Twelfth Night* in February 1602, and the next month he wrote down a story that he had heard about Burbage and Shakespeare. Burbage had seen a good-looking woman in the audience, and arranged to meet her. But Shakespeare had heard the conversation, and when Burbage knocked on her door, Shakespeare was already making love to her. Her servant gave Burbage a message from Shakespeare, saying 'William I (the first King of England) came before Richard III (Burbage's most famous part).'

The story is almost certainly not true. It is the kind of joke that students invent about famous people. But it shows that by this time they thought of Burbage and Shakespeare as stars. Although Shakespeare did not act the hero or the villain in his plays, people knew that he was one of the main reasons for his company's success. Students at Cambridge University had written a comedy about actors a year or two before this, and in that play the characters were Burbage, Kempe and Shakespeare.

◆

Between writing *Hamlet* and *Twelfth Night*, Shakespeare had had a lucky escape. His company had always supported the Earl of Essex, who was popular with the ordinary people, and the Earl of Southampton was Essex's closest friend. Essex had been a favourite at court for many years. Although he had annoyed the Queen and the government on several occasions, they gave him the command of the army when the Irish rebelled in 1599. Shakespeare included a speech in *Henry V*, comparing him to the hero of that play. But Essex failed. He was ordered to stay at home and keep away from the court.

Early in February 1601, one of his friends asked Shakespeare's company to perform *Richard II*, a play in which the King loses the throne. Essex and his friends wanted to see it before they rode to the Queen's palace. The actors agreed, but the next day Essex failed to get any popular support. He was sent to prison and executed a few days later. Southampton was lucky to escape with his life but stayed in prison until the Queen died in 1603.

Augustine Phillips, one of the actors, defended his friends at the trial. He said that they had only acted *Richard II* because they were offered more money. It is unlikely that the Queen believed him. She told one of the lords at court, 'I am Richard II. You know that, don't you?' But she did not punish the actors or the man who had written the play. Perhaps she was so fond of plays that she did not want to lose the best actors in the country. Instead, she warned them of the danger. They were ordered to perform at court on the night before Essex was executed.

Troilus and Cressida was the last play that Shakespeare wrote during the old queen's reign. It is a clever, cruel play, popular then and now with young people, and was probably first performed

The Earl of Southampton stayed in prison until 1603.

for the law students in London. The traditional characters, Hector and Troilus, have simple beliefs about love and war. But in the real world, Shakespeare suggests, neither love nor war is fair. In the end, people win by using force. Achilles murders Hector, and Cressida accepts Diomedes as her lover because she has never believed that love can last. The play is typical of attitudes in the last year of the old queen's reign. People looked back at the past sadly and were not confident about the future.

Towards the end of 1601, John Shakespeare died. He had lived long enough to see his son become the most successful man in Stratford. He left his two houses to William. Joan, William's sister, lived in one with her husband, and a man and his wife rented the other as a pub.

Chapter 8   Towards Tragedy

In February 1603, Queen Elizabeth died. Her nearest relative, James, King of Scotland, became King of England, too. Shakespeare's company had reason to be pleased. The Earl of Southampton came out of prison and soon became a favourite of the new king and queen. James decided to take personal control of the theatre companies. Only two were allowed to operate. Shakespeare's company became the King's Men; the other company was called the Queen's.

Shakespeare probably gave up acting at about this time. He had never played the main parts. According to later stories about him, he had a fine voice and usually took serious parts – kings, dukes or old men. In *Hamlet*, for example, he played the Ghost. There was a practical reason for this. Shakespeare was the director of his own plays, and the most difficult scenes are usually at the end when almost all the characters are on the stage. He needed to be off the stage to organize the other actors, so he usually played the part of a man who was dead or had disappeared before the end.

His next two plays, *All's Well that Ends Well* and *Measure for Measure*, are not completely successful. Shakespeare was still using stories from popular sources, but by this time his characters were too real to support the happy ending of a fairy story. *All's Well that Ends Well* does not end well. The nasty young hero, Bertram, who has refused to marry a girl from a lower social class, does not deserve her.

Measure for Measure has some wonderful scenes, but it annoys women today. The heroine, Isabella, refuses to sleep with the judge to save her brother's life but does not mind when another girl takes her place. We cannot accept this kind of solution to a problem if the characters seem real. But there was one advantage for Shakespeare in using this story by an Italian writer, Cinthio. In the same book, he found the story for his next play, *Othello*.

Shakespeare wrote three tragedies between 1604 and 1606, *Othello*, *King Lear* and *Macbeth*. If we compare them with his sources, we can understand their meaning from the changes that he made. Each of these three plays is great but the characters, the subject and the language are different. As always, he does not repeat his successes, but moves on to something new.

Like Hamlet, Othello is often misunderstood because people already have an idea of him in their minds when they come to the theatre. They suppose that he is a typical jealous husband. But this is the Othello of Cinthio's story, not of Shakespeare's play. Cinthio's characters do not have names, and the Moor★ and his wife are already married. An officer, who became Iago in Shakespeare's play, makes the Moor believe that his wife has slept with another officer, who became Cassio. The Moor and the

★Moor: a man from Morocco, but to Shakespeare and his audience a black man.

officer murder her together. There is a trial but neither of them is proved guilty. Afterwards, the wife's relatives kill the Moor, and the officer explains what really happened when he is in prison for another crime.

Shakespeare knew that jealous husbands usually belong to comedy, not tragedy. But Desdemona loves Othello so much that she dies saying that she killed herself. Before he introduced Cinthio's story, almost halfway through the play, Shakespeare had to show Othello as a great man and Othello and Desdemona as two people who are very much in love. This love is destroyed by the lies of a clever man, Iago. Shakespeare's audience were probably surprised by the scenes that he added at the beginning. Black men were usually shown as devils on the stage, not because people hated them in real life – they had probably never seen a black person – but because black was the Devil's colour. But in this play the Devil is white.

Shakespeare's attitude becomes clear if we realize that at this time he was living with a family of French Protestants, the Mountjoys. Protestants had suffered for their religious beliefs in France, but when some moved to England they were unpopular because they worked so hard. Just before he wrote *Othello*, Shakespeare was asked to write some scenes for a play about Sir Thomas More, Henry VIII's minister, who was executed because he did not agree to the king's marriage to Anne Boleyn. The play was never acted but we have a scene in Shakespeare's own writing. Sir Thomas asks a crowd of people in London who have been attacking foreigners: 'How would you feel if you went to a foreign country, like France, and people did not accept you as human beings?'

Othello defends himself at the end of the play, saying that he is not jealous by nature. Everyone in the play – even Emilia, his wife – believes that Iago is the honest soldier that he pretends to be. But Shakespeare shows us why Othello is tricked. He loves his beautiful young wife but he has never really understood why she loves him. She comes from one of the best families in Venice, but she has fallen in love with a black man, a foreigner, a man almost old enough to be her father. Although he is a great soldier, and the Venetians have given him command of their army, Othello has no experience of women.

In *Othello,* the love between husband and wife is destroyed. The next play, *King Lear*, is about parents and children. There was an old play about King Lear that we can compare with Shakespeare's. The story also appeared in 'histories' of Britain, although there was no real King Lear.

In all the sources, Lear was an old king with three daughters, two bad and one good. He decided to divide the country between them equally, but he asked them to tell him which of them loved him most. Two daughters made long speeches, saying how much they loved him, but the third (in Shakespeare's play, Cordelia) did not. King Lear was angry and sent her away, but found that the older daughters were cruel to him when she had gone.

In Shakespeare's play the two older daughters are married, so they have to say that they love their father more than their husbands. Lear goes mad and, in his madness, discovers that he is not a king but only a man. For comparison, Shakespeare also used another story by Sir Philip Sidney about a man with one good son and one bad one, and gave the father the name of Gloucester. Finally, in all the sources, there is a happy ending.

Gloucester dies happily in the arms of his good son. This is the kind of ending that we can expect in stories. But the ending of Lear's story shows us a world where there is no God to save us from suffering. In this world we can only believe in human love. And this is not enough to save us from dying, or, even worse, to save the lives of the people that we love.

Lear comes on to the stage at the end of the play carrying the dead body of Cordelia in his arms. We realize then that it does

King Lear carries the dead body of Cordelia in his arms.

not matter who is king or queen or who has political power in the country. Lear's best-loved child is dead, and he can do nothing to change that.

At such moments, most dramatists of Shakespeare's time wrote long speeches for the actor. But Shakespeare always uses simple language in scenes like these. He wanted to make sure that everyone in the audience understood what was happening. And so King Lear, before he dies of a broken heart, says that he will never see his daughter again: 'Never, never, never, never, never.'

Perhaps in this play Shakespeare showed how he felt about the death of his only son.

The patron of Shakespeare's company was now a Scottish king, and so *Macbeth*, the third great tragedy, was probably written to please him. The story is taken from a history of Scotland, and James I believed that he belonged to the family of one of the characters, Banquo. When Shakespeare began to write about a hero who becomes a villain, he was probably thinking of the lucky escape that James had had on 5 November 1605. Some Catholics tried to kill him with an explosion under the Houses of Parliament. The Earl of Southampton and the brothers of two of Shakespeare's friends were there. The date is still celebrated in Britain every year as Guy Fawkes' Day.

When Shakespeare began writing plays, characters alone on the stage spoke to the audience mainly to tell them what was going to happen. But by the time he wrote *Macbeth*, he could show the hero's mind working. Before and after Macbeth murders the King, we hear him thinking about his actions. In this way, we can see how he realizes that one crime leads to another. He never feels guilty about anything that he has done, but we are unable to look away from the stage because of the power and beauty of the language.

Shakespeare's speeches, in his greatest plays, suit the character who is speaking and come naturally from what is happening on the stage. In plays like *Macbeth* we remember the lines because of the pictures that Shakespeare paints in our minds. Halfway through the play, Macbeth decides to kill the wife and children of his enemy, Macduff. 'Why not?' he asks himself. He imagines that he is halfway across a river of blood. It is so deep that he would feel as tired if he went back as if he crossed over to the other side. He does not feel guilty. By now, another crime is just something that makes him tired, not something that he is sorry for.

Macbeth and the later tragedies show that Shakespeare, like other Elizabethan dramatists, thought that tragedy simply meant the fall of a great man. The man did not need to be good. Most audiences admire Hamlet and feel sorry for Othello and King Lear, but Macbeth is a villain. Shakespeare's opinion of him and of all political leaders like him is clear from the words that he puts into Macbeth's own mouth at the end. Macbeth realizes that after all his crimes, he has none of the things that people look forward to when they grow old – love, friends, the knowledge that people admire them. The people around him only obey him because they are afraid.

Chapter 9   Romans, Greeks and a Wedding

Shakespeare returned to Roman history for the subjects of his next three plays. *Julius Caesar* had been successful a few years earlier, so the company probably thought that it would be a good idea to continue the story. Shakespeare's source for that play had been the Greek historian, Plutarch, who wrote in the second century. There was a very good translation of his work in English, which Shakespeare used. So towards the end of 1606 or early in 1607, he wrote the first of these plays, *Antony and Cleopatra*.

In Shakespeare's time, people thought that the Romans were the most important people who had ever lived. Latin was not needed in Protestant churches, but boys still studied it at school so they could read Roman literature. The work of writers like Plutarch helped them form their ideas about society and politics. Above all, they were interested in the lives of great men like Julius Caesar and Mark Antony.

Shakespeare followed his source more closely than in other plays. But he did not always share Plutarch's opinion of the characters, and by this time he was able to turn the excellent translation into the form of language that was best for the subject. For this reason, the language of *Antony and Cleopatra*, a play about two of the most famous lovers in the history of the world, is perhaps the finest and most romantic that he ever wrote.

Cleopatra's wonderful speeches make it a very difficult part for an actress. There were no actresses in the theatre at that time, so all the women's parts were played by boys. It is hard to believe that a boy appeared as Cleopatra. But Shakespeare always wrote with his company in mind. In comedies like *As You Like It* and *Twelfth Night*, the story gave him the excuse to dress the heroine in boy's clothes for most of the play and so the boy could use his own voice. But Lady Macbeth, Cleopatra and Volumnia, the hero's mother in *Coriolanus*, are much older women. It seems likely that between 1606 and 1608, there was a boy in the company with the ability to play such parts.

Shakespeare shows that he is confident in the actors by reminding the audience that they are seeing a play. When Brutus and Cassius have killed Caesar in *Julius Caesar*, Cassius says that the scene of the murder will be acted in countries (like England) that do not yet exist and in languages (like English) that are not yet known.

In *Antony and Cleopatra*, Shakespeare is even more daring. Cleopatra realizes after Antony's death that Octavius will take her to Rome and show her to the ordinary people. Actors, she says, will make fun of her and of Antony, and she will see a boy with a

Antony and Cleopatra *is a play about two of the most famous lovers in the history of the world.*

high voice playing the part of Cleopatra and making her, a great queen, look cheap.

Some writers have imagined that when he wrote this, Shakespeare was apologizing to the audience. It can be argued, though, that the opposite is true. He was so sure of himself and the actors that, at the most important moments in the play, he was saying: 'We are good enough to show you the greatest people who have ever lived.'

Today people have very different opinions about *Antony and Cleopatra*. Romantics would like to give the play the title that John Dryden gave his play about the lovers some years later – *All for Love (or the World Well Lost)*. Others see it as mainly political – like Plutarch, who said that Antony's relationship with Cleopatra destroyed him. This second group cannot understand why Shakespeare allows Cleopatra to compare Antony to Octavius, his rival for power in Rome, at the end of the play and to say that Octavius's success means nothing. Shakespeare is suggesting that greatness is a personal quality that Antony had and Octavius will never have.

Shakespeare does not take sides in the argument. He knew from his own experience that in politics the cool head of a man like Octavius will always beat the warm, generous heart of a man like Antony. He had seen this happen when Lord Burghley's son, Cecil, was too clever for the more popular Earl of Essex.

The play is really about being a star. For Shakespeare and his audience stars were not, as they are today, actors, pop singers and footballers. They were people with power – kings and queens, lords and ladies. It is interesting that when Antony believes that Cleopatra is dead and decides to kill himself, he imagines that the two of them will meet again after death. He is not looking forward to making love for ever. It is important for him that the other great lovers in history will recognize them as the greatest of all.

In the same way, Cleopatra kills herself at the end of the play because this proves that she is a queen. She will not let any ordinary person have the opportunity to destroy her. We do not feel sorry for Antony and Cleopatra at the end of the play as we do when young lovers like Romeo and Juliet die. We can only admire them because the truly great are beyond pity.

After this, Shakespeare probably worked on another story from Plutarch, *Timon of Athens*. The play seems unfinished, and there is no report of a performance in his lifetime. In the story of Timon the Greek general, Alcibiades, appears. In the war between Athens and Sparta, Alcibiades was driven out of Athens and in revenge led a Spartan army against it. But when Shakespeare decided to write a play about a man like that, he chose a similar story about a Roman, Coriolanus, instead.

Coriolanus is Shakespeare's most political play. In it he compares the attitudes of different social classes, and so most readers today understand it according to their own political beliefs. This is a mistake because society has changed so much since Shakespeare's time – and had already changed when he wrote the play in comparison with the Rome of his source.

When Rome was still a small city state, fighting against its neighbours, it needed a special group of professional soldiers in time of war. They were similar to the men in films about Japanese history like *The Seven Samurai*. In the play, Coriolanus is the bravest of them. At the end of a war, men like these were often chosen to govern the city in peacetime. Coriolanus is proud and has no political skill. The ordinary people's leaders attack him; they do not need him now, and he is not willing to tell lies to get their votes. In his opinion, only people from his own class, who have fought for the city, should have the right to vote.

None of the characters in *Coriolanus* is admirable. Shakespeare gives the people a better reason for disliking Coriolanus than Plutarch did, but shows that they are easily tricked. In all his plays, ordinary people are generally kind and sensible, but when they form a crowd, they stop thinking and become violent. In some ways Coriolanus himself is like Antony and Timon. They are all men who do not obey the customs of their society and in the end are destroyed for this reason.

We can only guess Shakespeare's own political views. But they were probably the same as the views of the parliamentary leaders who rebelled against the King forty years later and executed him in 1649. Unlike the King, they believed that the people should have the right to choose their leaders. But they also believed that only property owners should vote because other people had nothing to lose. Shakespeare, who owned quite a lot of property, almost certainly agreed.

◆

During this time, there were two important events in Shakespeare's private life. In June 1607 his older daughter, Susanna, married Dr John Hall. Susanna was now twenty-four and her husband was thirty-two. Hall had studied at Cambridge University and moved to Stratford a few years earlier. He became well known in the medical profession, using plants to cure his patients. He was a serious man and almost certainly the most intelligent in Stratford, except for Shakespeare himself. It is clear that Shakespeare liked him and was pleased that his favourite daughter had found such a good husband. From this time, the main subject of his plays is the relationship between parents and children, especially between fathers and daughters.

Shakespeare was probably serious about his responsibilities as a father and was probably a better father than he was a husband or son. Some writers have suggested that when he invented powerful female characters like Volumnia, Coriolanus's mother, he was thinking of his own mother, Mary Arden. She died in September 1608. Perhaps he waited until after her death before publishing his Sonnets the following year because he was unwilling to let her know the details of his private life.

Chapter 10   Return to Stratford

Many years earlier, in 1596, James Burbage had rented a hall in London. Although the actors continued to act at the Globe Theatre, they preferred to work indoors. Shakespeare was again one of the partners when they opened the Blackfriars theatre in 1608. The other great advantage of a second theatre for the company was that in future they could act in London in winter as well as in summer. Until then, they had only acted at court at Christmas time or in special performances for the law students.

At this time, a new kind of play was coming into fashion. The rival company to Shakespeare's had performed an old play called *Mucedorus* with great success in 1607. Two years later, two young dramatists, Francis Beaumont and John Fletcher, wrote *Philaster*, a play that Fletcher described as mixing tragedy and comedy. These plays were taken from popular stories, like Shakespeare's romantic comedies, but the stories were more serious at first; they began like a tragedy but had a happy ending.

Shakespeare, as always, noticed changes in fashion. Early in 1608, he worked on a play called *Pericles*. He never wrote anything as bad as the scenes at the beginning. But suddenly, almost halfway through, the style changes. The rest of the play is typical of Shakespeare at this time. It seems that a man called George Wilkins wrote the early scenes and Shakespeare finished the play. It was not included in his collected works in 1623, so it is clear that his friends, who acted with him, knew that he had not written all of it.

In *Pericles* the hero is separated from his wife and daughter; he believes that they are dead, but meets them again. Their meeting is one of Shakespeare's finest scenes, but the play is difficult because the first half is so different from the second.

Shakespeare's next play of this type, *Cymbeline*, is also rather confused. He was probably not completely satisfied with it, and as usual when he had not succeeded, he returned to the same subject. In the third play, *The Winter's Tale*, written in 1610, he manages to solve the problem of a play that begins like a tragedy but has a happy ending.

The title of this play means a fairy story, the kind of story that people tell in winter to pass the time. The play is about forgiveness for the past, and there are a number of things in it that seem to be connected with Shakespeare's own life. The source is an old story by Robert Greene, the man who had attacked Shakespeare when he first succeeded as a dramatist. Greene's story ends sadly, but Shakespeare changed the ending to write the kind of play that Beaumont and Fletcher had described.

Leontes, the King of Sicily, has always been friendly with the King of Bohemia, Polixenes. Leontes is Shakespeare's idea of a jealous man. Othello only becomes jealous when Iago tricks him. But Leontes imagines a relationship between his wife, Hermione, and Polixenes for no reason.

After Polixenes has been staying at his court for some time, Leontes suddenly decides that Hermione's unborn child is Polixenes's, not his. Polixenes escapes, but when the baby girl is born Leontes orders one of his lords, Antigonus, to take it to another country and leave it for wild animals to eat. He puts Hermione on trial, acting as the judge himself, and says that she is guilty. He has sent two men to ask the god Apollo for advice, but he does not wait for them to return. When they do, they bring the message that Hermione is innocent. At this point another messenger comes in to say that the young prince, Mamillius, has died, afraid of what will happen to his mother. Hermione falls to the ground and is carried out of the court. Paulina, Antigonus's wife, comes back to tell Leontes that she is dead, too.

We see Antigonus with the baby in Bohemia, Polixenes's country, and there is an amusing moment when an animal comes on the stage and Antigonus runs away. An old man finds the baby and tells the audience that the animal has eaten Antigonus.

Before the next scene, an actor tells the audience that sixteen years have passed. The baby has grown up into a beautiful young girl called Perdita (which means 'lost') and the young prince, Polixenes's son, is in love with her. His father is very angry but the young couple escape to Sicily. There Leontes helps them and, in the end, the old man brings some letters that he kept. These prove that she is Leontes's daughter. The young couple are married, and finally, we learn that Hermione did not die. Paulina looked after her. So Leontes finds his wife and daughter again after many years.

When he wrote this play, Shakespeare was living in Stratford again for most of the year. If it tells us something about his own life, we may suppose that he became jealous of his wife while he was absent in London many years earlier. But Susanna's marriage to Dr Hall had helped him to discover happiness again with his family. We cannot prove that this is true but it is interesting that at the end of *The Winter's Tale*, when everyone is happy, no one says anything about the young prince, Mamillius. In the play, he died sixteen years earlier, almost the same length of time in 1610 since the death of Shakespeare's own son, Hamnet.

Chapter 11   Last Years

Shakespeare still belonged to the King's Men, and in 1611 he wrote the last play that is completely his own work, *The Tempest*. It is another play about forgiveness and, as in *The Winter's Tale*, the happy ending is produced by a marriage between the children of two men who are enemies.

In this play, Shakespeare found a different solution to the problem of time passing. Instead of having a break of sixteen years in the middle of the play, Prospero, the main character, explains to his daughter, Miranda, how they arrived on the island where they live. Prospero was the Duke of Milan but when Miranda was a baby, his brother Antonio, with the help of the King of Naples, rebelled against him. Prospero was put into a boat with the baby and came to the island. But he brought his books with him, and as a result of studying them he now has magic power. Before this scene, we have seen all his enemies on a ship in a storm. Prospero says that he caused the storm because he wanted to bring them to the island.

The play is complicated for many people today for two reasons. First, Prospero has a servant, Caliban, who is half human and lived on the island before he arrived. Prospero was kind to him until he attacked Miranda. Second, Shakespeare invented this story himself but included details from a report of a voyage to America by a man called Strachey. At that time, the English were trying to build a town in Virginia. Some modern directors see Prospero as the villain, not the hero, connecting Caliban with Native Americans.* But Shakespeare's island, as the characters' names suggest, is in the Mediterranean, not far from Italy, and the subject of the play is forgiveness.

Many writers have imagined that Prospero is Shakespeare himself. Towards the end of the play he makes a speech forgiving his enemies and promising not to use magic again. This was the last play that Shakespeare wrote by himself. He had used the magic of words for many years but perhaps he had now decided, like Prospero, to return to his family. There his strength, as Prospero says, would be his own. This may be partly true, but Shakespeare took Prospero's speech about magic from a speech made by Medea in his favourite Latin poem, Ovid's *Metamorphoses*.

---

*Native Americans: the people who lived in the United States before the Europeans arrived.

Prospero has a servant, Caliban, who is half human.

In fact, he continued to write for two more years with the help of John Fletcher, who took his place as the main dramatist for the King's Men. Only one of these plays, *Henry VIII*, appears in his collected works. Shakespeare was still a partner in the company, but in 1613 the Globe theatre burned down during a performance of *Henry VIII*, and after that it seems that he ended his connection with them.

◆

Shakespeare lived quietly in Stratford until 1616, but in March of that year he became ill. He died a month later, on 23 April, just after his fifty-second birthday. There has been a lot of discussion about his will, especially because he only left his wife the 'second-best bed'. It seems that he first made his will in January 1616, but did not sign it at that time and changed it when he realized that he was dying.

In that time he had a very worrying experience. His second daughter, Judith, who was then thirty-one, married a man called Thomas Quiney on 10 February. Shakespeare's family had known the Quiney family for many years. But a month later another woman, Margaret Wheeler, died giving birth to a child and Quiney was named as the father. When he signed his will on 25 March, Shakespeare clearly thought about this.

He left almost everything to his older daughter, Susanna. She and her husband, Dr Hall, were given responsibility for the will. He was probably afraid that his wife's relatives, the Hathaway family, would come to her for money, and Judith's husband, Quiney, was clearly not a good man. He did not leave 'the second-best bed' to Anne as an insult to his wife, but as a memory of their marriage. It was the bed that they slept in. They kept the best bed for guests!

Chapter 12 'Not of an age but for all time'

Shakespeare remembered a number of his friends with small gifts in his will, but only three of them were members of his company: the great actor Richard Burbage, John Heminges and Henry Condell. Burbage died in 1619. The other two are the men who made it possible for us to see and read Shakespeare's plays today.

At that time, few people thought of plays as literature. When Ben Jonson published his collected works in 1616, the year of Shakespeare's death, people made a joke about it. They said that Jonson did not know the difference between 'work' and 'play'. So Heminges and Condell did not expect to make much money from publishing Shakespeare's plays in the same way. They did it as a duty in memory of their friend. Eighteen of Shakespeare's thirty-seven plays appeared for the first time in the collected works published in 1623. They included some of his finest tragedies and comedies – *Macbeth*, *Antony and Cleopatra*, *As You Like It* and *Twelfth Night*.

Ben Jonson often criticized Shakespeare's work in private conversations. He was a great dramatist himself, but he wrote a different kind of play. But for Heminges and Condell's complete works, he wrote a fine poem about his friend and rival. He compared him to the best of the Greek and Roman dramatists and said that Shakespeare was the greatest of them all: 'He was not of an age but for all time.' (He did not only belong to his own time. His work will live for ever.)

All writers belong to the time when they live. It is a mistake to imagine that Shakespeare had the same views on religion or politics as we have. No serious student accepts that, and it is a pity that so many modern directors change the meaning of his plays in performance to suit their own opinions. So Jonson was right that Shakespeare was not only a man of his own time. But he was also right in the sense that Shakespeare's plays give pleasure to people at all times and help them to understand life better.

This is partly because the plays are full of exciting scenes and wonderful speeches, and the characters are still real for us because they have a special way of speaking that suits them personally. Shakespeare was never satisfied with one form of play, and so almost all of his plays contain something new and different. He studied the successes of other dramatists and improved on them. Finally, he was a great dramatist because he was an actor. In some of his sonnets, he seems ashamed of his profession. He wanted to be known as a gentleman. But his plays are great because he always imagined them on the stage while he was writing and he knew which actor was going to play each part.

But Shakespeare's great ability in the theatre is only part of the story. *King Lear* is a play that asks the question: 'What is a man?' In this play, Lear realizes that titles like King or Lord are not the things that matter in life. He learns that ordinary people suffer in the same way as he does and that before everything else, a man is a father, son or husband.

Shakespeare understood the minds of men and women and can help us to understand them. Because he was an actor and spent his life studying people and listening to them, he could imagine the thoughts and emotions of all kinds of men and women. He can make us believe that he knew what an old Jewish person or a black soldier thought, although he had probably never spoken to one. He can show us the hopes and fears of an intelligent young girl or an Egyptian queen, although in his lifetime these parts were always acted by boys.

And so if you are fortunate enough to see a great Shakespeare play well acted, this is still the most wonderful experience that you can have in a theatre.

William Shakespeare

ACTIVITIES

Chapters 1–4

Before you read

1 Write down everything you know about Shakespeare. Can you name any of his plays or characters? Have you read or seen any plays? Compare your answers with another student's.

2 Find these words in your dictionary and answer the questions.

audience council director dramatist earl patron poet rival villain

Which is a word for a person who

  a writes plays?   **e** is in competition with you?

  b writes poems?   **f** is the bad man in a play?

  c makes films?   **g** helps writers or actors?

  d is a lord?

Which is a word for a group of people who

  h control a town?

  i watch a play?

3 Find these words in your dictionary.

comedy plague sonnet source tragedy will

Which is a word for:

  a a play that ends happily?

  b a play that ends unhappily?

  c a short poem?

  d an important document?

  e a terrible illness?

  f a story that another writer uses?

4 Find these words in your dictionary. Use them to complete the sentences below. Choose the correct verb form.

divide execute publish rebel reign revenge throne

  a When lords . . . . . against the Queen and tried to put her cousin on the . . . . . , they were . . . .

  b During her long . . . . . , Queen Elizabeth took . . . . . on many of her enemies.

  c If you . . . . . this book in two, it can be . . . . . in two parts.

After you read

5 Why do you think Stratford-upon-Avon is popular with tourists? What do they visit while they are there?

6 Work with another student. Have this conversation.

Student A: You are William Shakespeare. Tell your father that you want to marry Anne, and answer his questions.

Student B: You are John Shakespeare. Why don't you want William to marry her? Why do you give him your permission?

7 In what ways was the theatre in London in 1590 like Hollywood in the 1930s?

Chapters 5–8

Before you read

8 Discuss these questions. Find the words in *italics* in your dictionary.

a How do you think a family gets a *coat of arms*?

b Do you prefer *comic* plays, or tragedies? Why?

c Are these usually good or bad characters in a play?
   the Devil   duke   fairy   heroine

d When should a judge show *mercy* after a *trial*?

After you read

9 Why did Shakespeare write *The Merry Wives of Windsor* and *The Merchant of Venice*?

10 Imagine that you are Richard Burbage and you have seen a modern theatre. What differences do you notice?

11 Act out this conversation.

Student A: You are the judge at the trial of the Earl of Essex. Tell the Queen why the actors acted *Richard II* for him.

Student B: You are Queen Elizabeth. You do not believe the actors. Say what you think and what you are going to do.

Chapters 9–12

Before you read

12 Which of these characters in Shakespeare's plays have you heard or read about? What do you know about them? Compare your ideas with the ideas of other students.

Antony Cleopatra Coriolanus Prospero

After you read

13 Answer these questions.

   a What ideas did the Elizabethans have about the Romans? Which characters interested them most and why?

   b What does *The Winter's Tale* seem to tell us about Shakespeare's relationship with his family?

14 Act out this conversation.

   Student A: You are Shakespeare. You are very ill and are going to make your will. Tell Anne what you are going to do.

   Student B: You are his wife. Ask him why he is leaving almost everything to Susanna, and very little to you.

Writing

15 You are Shakespeare. Write a letter to Anne sometime between the years 1585 and 1592. Say what you have been doing and ask for news of the family.

16 You are John Manningham. You have just seen a Shakespeare play and heard a story about the dramatist. Write your diary.

17 Write a conversation between Shakespeare and John Hall. Hall has come to see him because he wants to marry Susanna.

18 Which of Shakespeare's plays would you like to see or read? Why? What have you learnt about it?

Answers for the activities in this book are available from your local Pearson Education office or contact: Penguin Readers Marketing Department, Pearson Education, Edinburgh Gate, Harlow, Essex, CM20 2JE.